MAKE AND COLOUR

CARS & TRUCKS

Clare Beaton

b small publishing

How to use this book

First remove the centre black and white pages of the book. These are vehicles ready for you to colour in and make. Place the book on a flat surface and ask an adult to help you open the staples. Carefully pull out the centre pages, then close the staples again.

First of all, colour the vehicles. Use coloured pencils, crayons, felt-tip pens or paints. (Use fairly thick paint and wash your brush between colours.) Leave the pages flat to dry.

Follow the instructions below for how to make the vehicles.

Keep the rest of the book. It has lots of ideas on how to create traffic scenes to play with. There are also templates and stencils to help you, and on the inside back cover you'll find ideas for games to play with your vehicles.

Some things you will need:
- ❏ plain and coloured paper or thick card
- ❏ thick card, card tubes and boxes
- ❏ sticky tape and glue
- ❏ scissors and craft knife
- ❏ tracing paper, pencil and ruler
- ❏ crayons, paints and felt-tip pens
- ❏ skewer or darning needle
- ❏ fun fur fabric
- ❏ string
- ❏ plasticine
- ❏ drinking straws
- ❏ sticky shapes

This symbol is to remind you to ask an adult to help when you use a craft knife.

Making the vehicles on the centre pages

First separate the vehicles: cut along the straight lines where it says 'CUT'.

Now you have the two sides of each vehicle, with a dotted fold line down the middle. Score carefully along the fold, using a ruler and the point of some scissors. Fold along the line.

Next, open out the shape and glue inside, then fold shut.

To make your vehicles a bit stiffer, slip some thin card inside (e.g. from a cereal packet) before you glue it shut.

Lastly, cut out the vehicle and cut the slot where marked on each one.

Make a stand for each vehicle using the templates on the first centre page. Slot a stand on to each vehicle, and off you go!

Templates

Here is a way to trace simply and successfully from the templates on the inside front cover.

What you will need:
- ❒ tracing paper
- ❒ soft pencil
- ❒ sticky tape
- ❒ paper or card

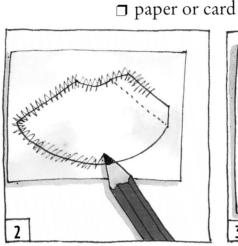

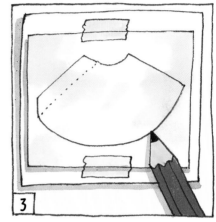

Tape a piece of tracing paper over the template. Trace one of the shapes with the pencil.

Turn over the tracing paper and scribble over the lines with the pencil.

Turn over again and tape on to some card or paper. Retrace firmly over the lines. Remove the tracing paper.

Stencils

Cut or tear off the sheet of stencils from the back cover. Follow the instructions below on how to use them.

What you will need:
- ❒ paper or card (coloured if you want)
- ❒ pencil
- ❒ scissors

Place the stencil shape on some card or paper. Draw inside the shape with a pencil.

Colour in the outline shape or cut it out with scissors.

Loads of roads

Make a mega road layout for all your vehicles.

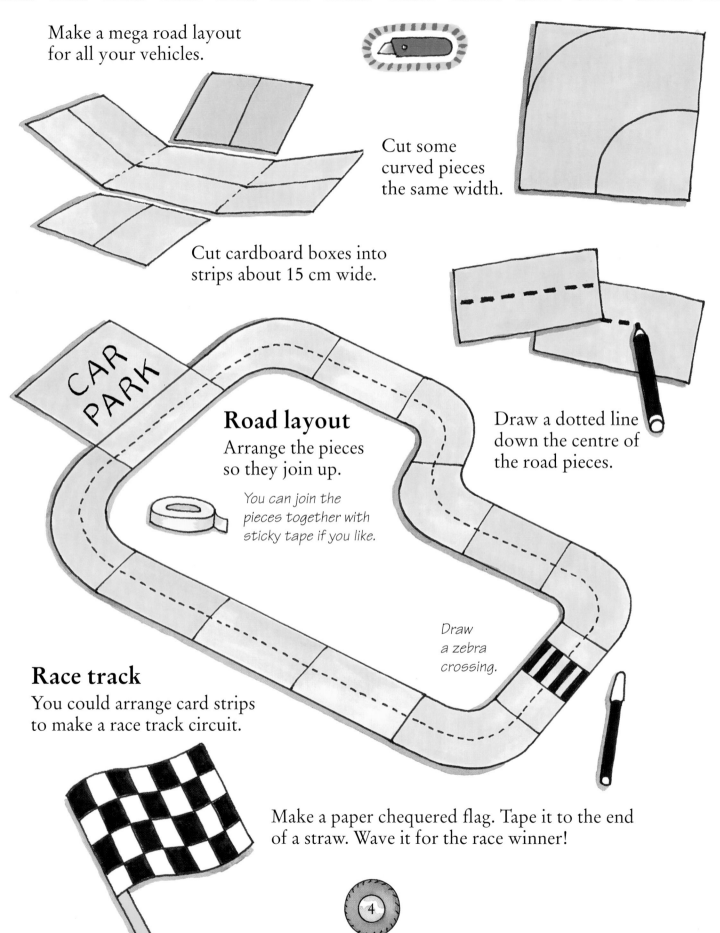

Cut cardboard boxes into strips about 15 cm wide.

Cut some curved pieces the same width.

Draw a dotted line down the centre of the road pieces.

CAR PARK

Road layout
Arrange the pieces so they join up.

You can join the pieces together with sticky tape if you like.

Draw a zebra crossing.

Race track
You could arrange card strips to make a race track circuit.

Make a paper chequered flag. Tape it to the end of a straw. Wave it for the race winner!

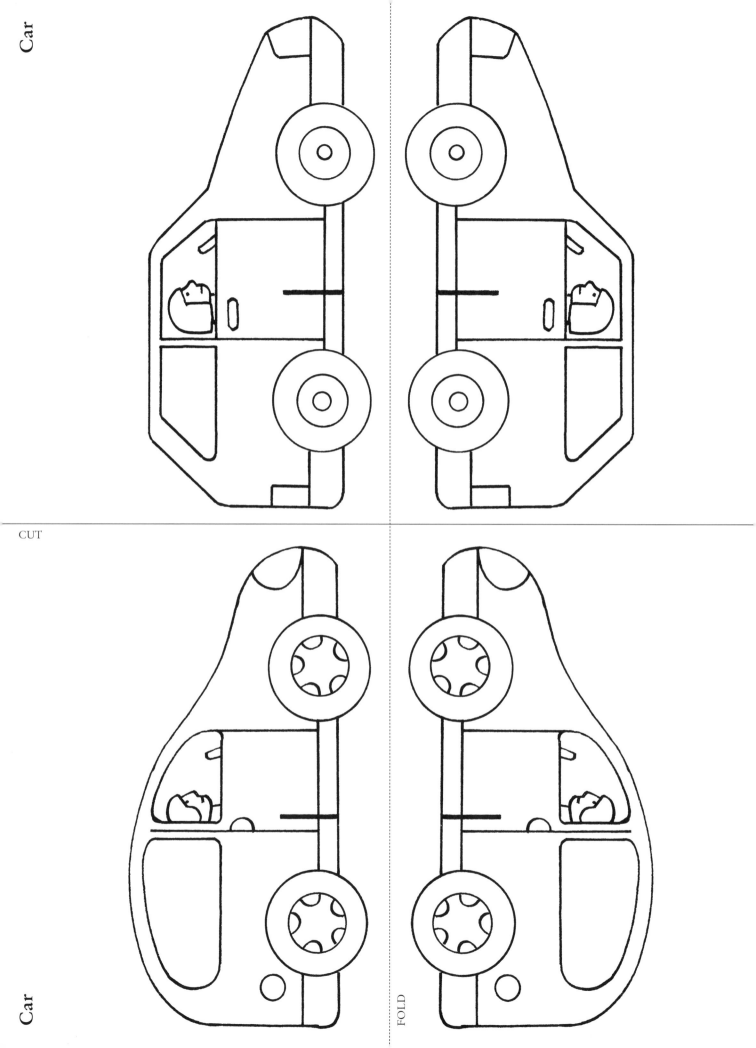

CUT

FOLD

Truck

CUT

Racing car

Racing car

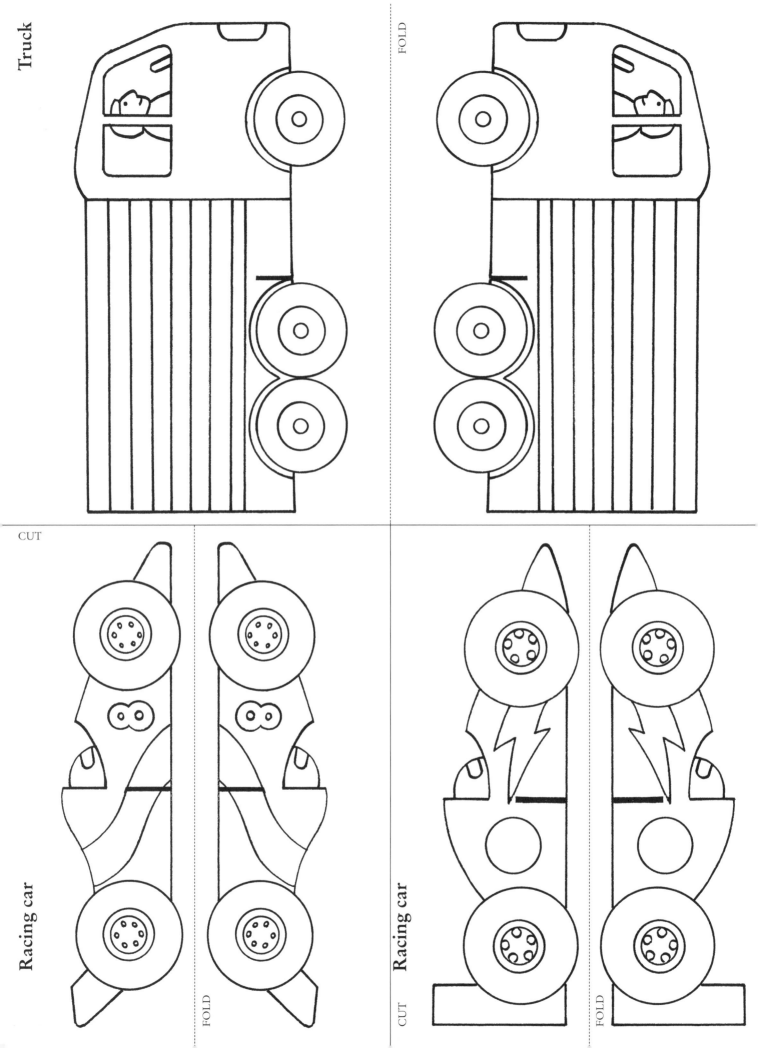

FOLD

CUT

FOLD

CUT

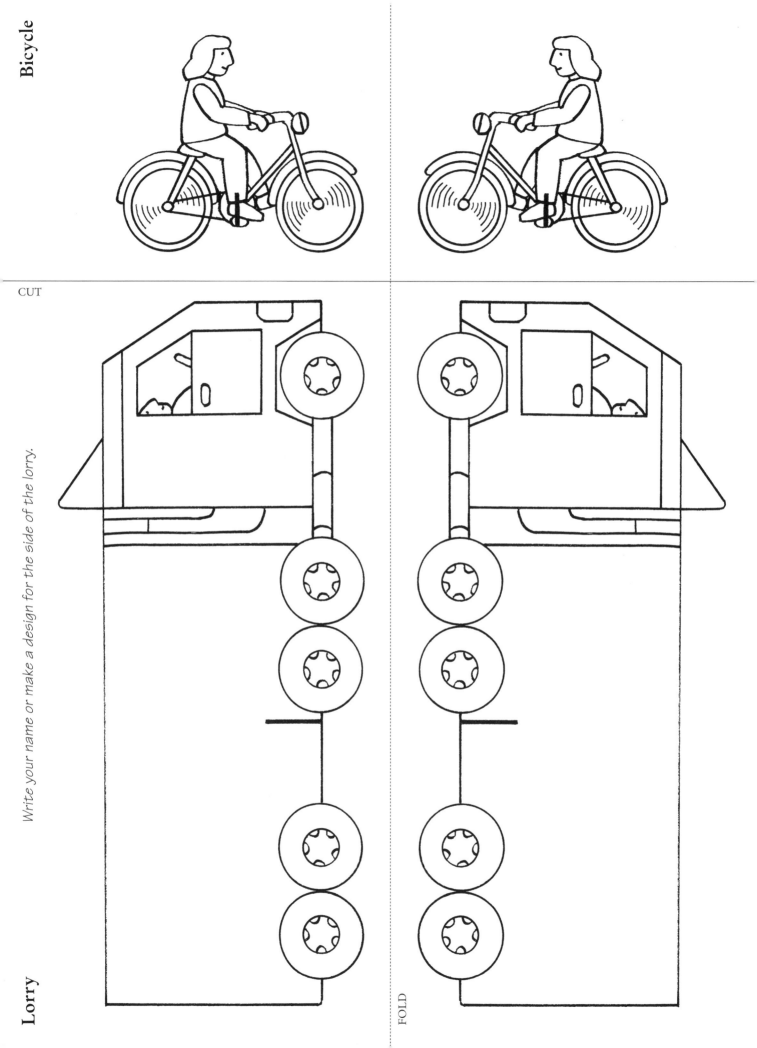

Write your name or make a design for the side of the lorry.

Lorry

FOLD

Cars and trucks and things that go

Follow the instructions on page 2 to colour and make the vehicles on these pages.

Make a stand for each vehicle using these templates (see page 3 for instructions).

Stand template

Small stand template

Use the small stand for the racing cars, motorbike and bicycle, and the large stand for everything else.

CUT

Bus

FOLD

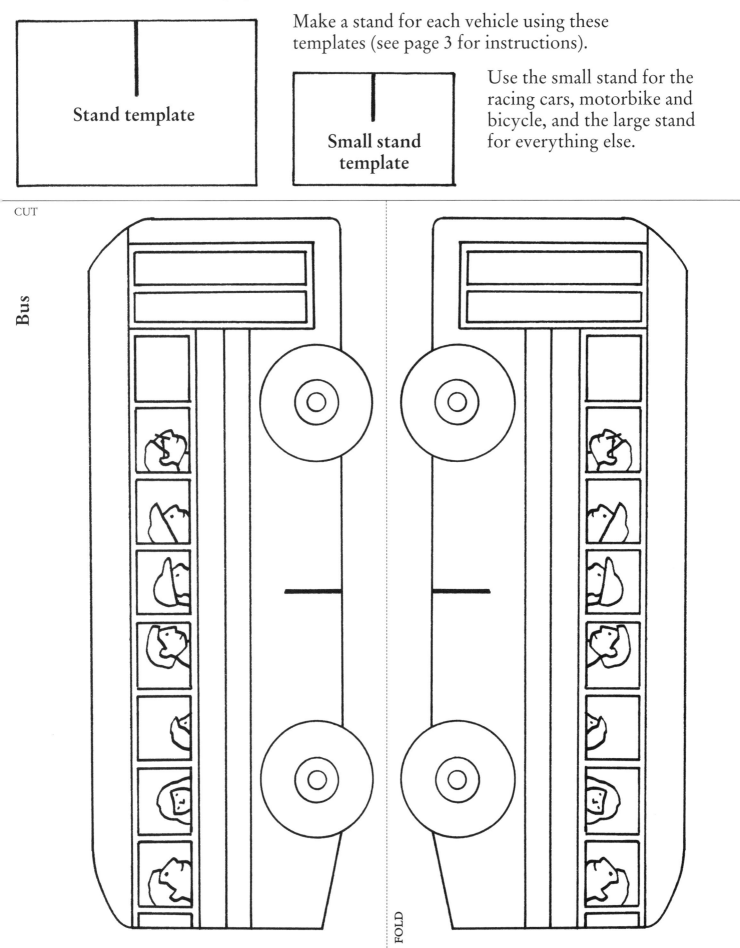

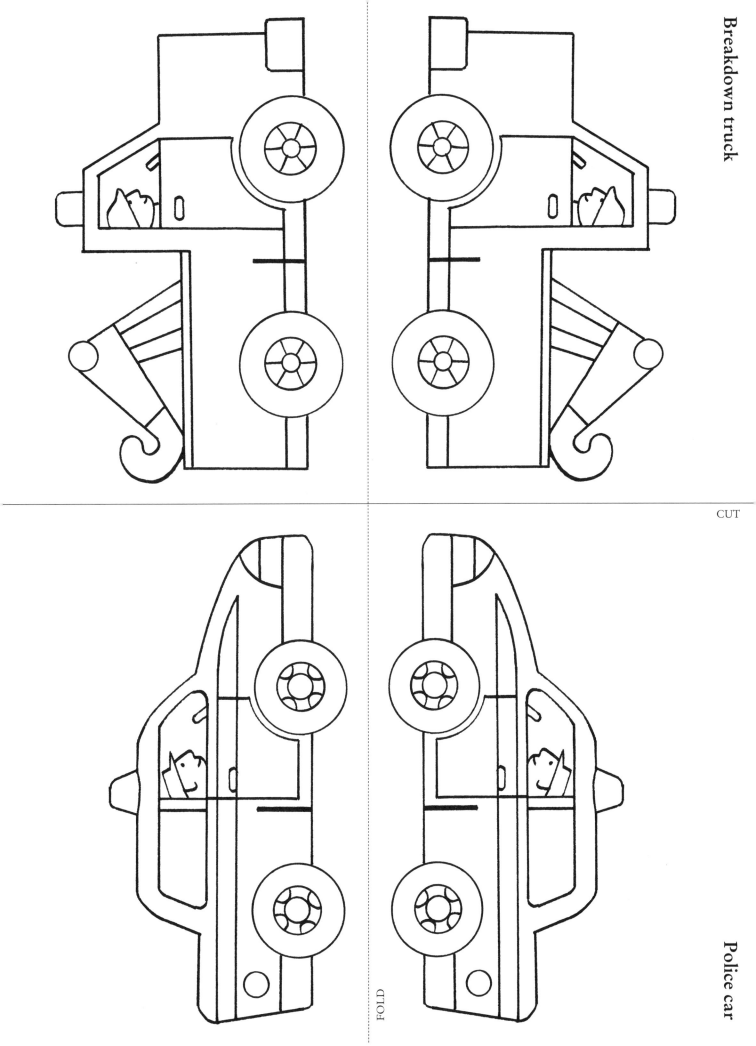

CUT

FOLD

CUT

FOLD

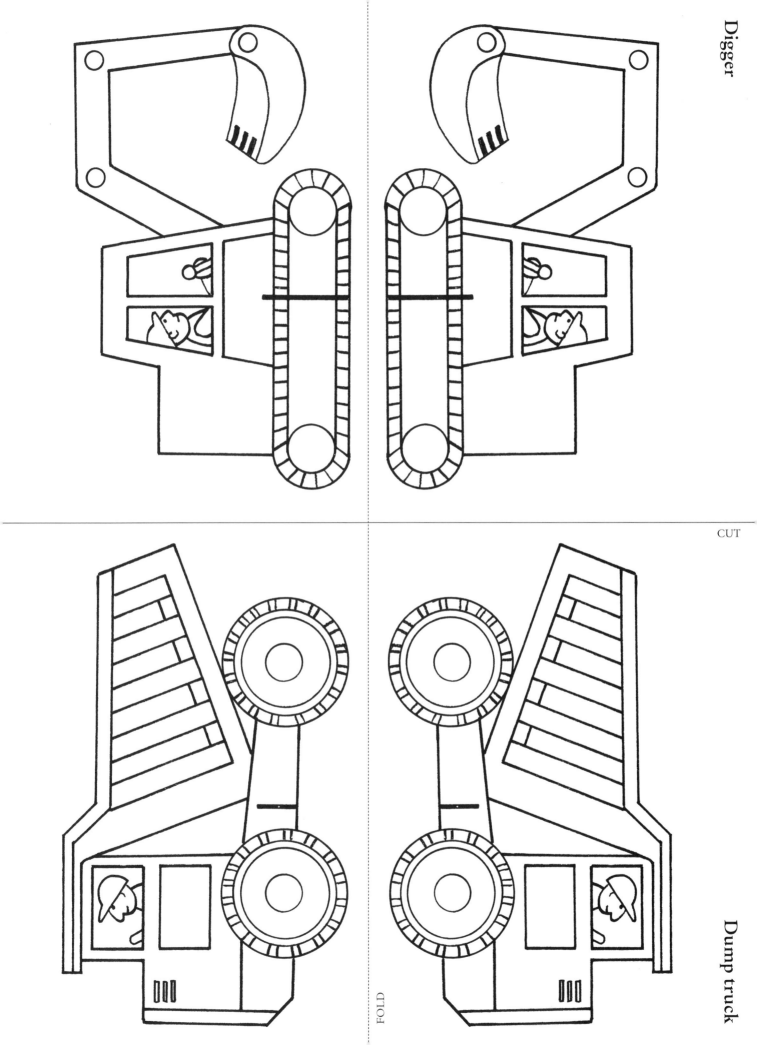

CUT

FOLD

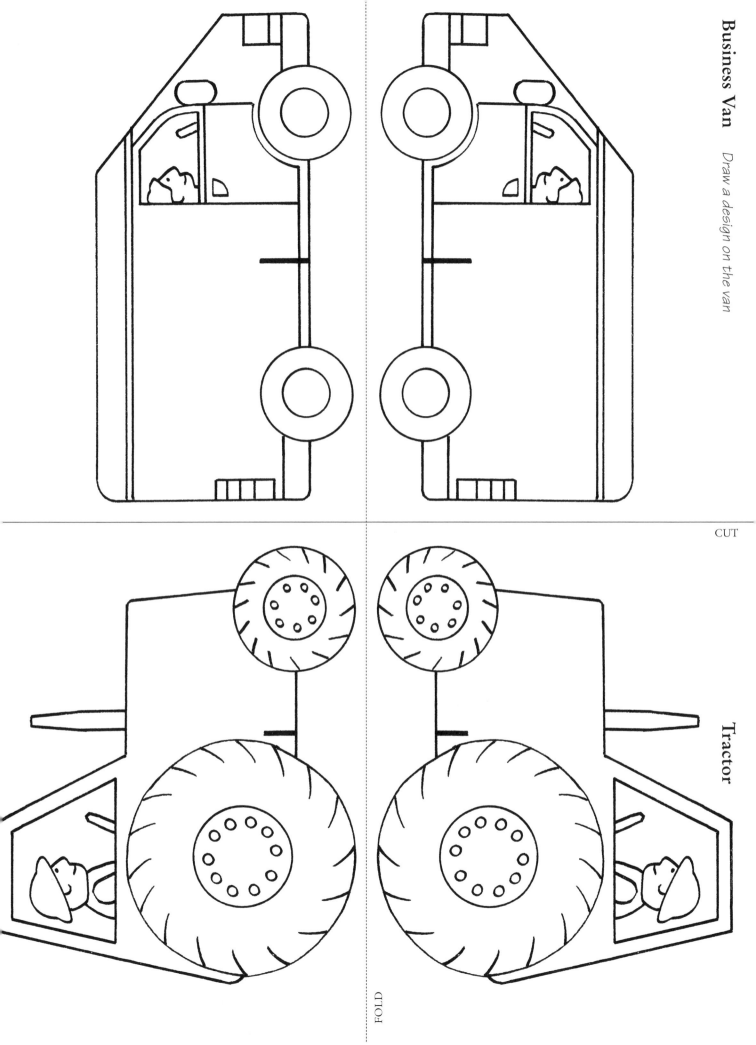

Draw a design on the van

CUT

Tractor

FOLD

Road barrier

Trace the barrier template below (see page 3 for help) and cut out four pieces. Cut the slit where shown, and slot two of the pieces together. Do the same with the other two. Use striped straws or paint stripes on a straw and place it between the two stands.

Barrier template

Traffic cones and lights

Use the templates on the inside front cover and instructions on page 3 to make these. Colour the lights red, amber (orange) and green. Colour the cones with red or orange and white stripes.

Road signs and bus stops

Cut circles, squares and triangles out of stiff paper or card. Draw and write on both sides.

Cut a slit down one end of a straw and push a sign into it. Stick the other end into a blob of plasticine.

Place your signs along the road layout.

Road work sign
Colour one side green and write GO. Make the other side red and write STOP.

5

Garage

Take the lids off two shoe boxes (or similar boxes).
Arrange the boxes on their sides, facing opposite ways, as in the picture below. Glue them together.

Draw the garage door and window.
Write the signs on the walls.

Petrol pumps

Remove the match drawer from an empty box of household matches. Cover the outside sleeve with coloured paper.

Make two holes in one side of the box with a pointed instrument (e.g. pencil or skewer).

Cut a 10-cm length of string and push one end through one of the holes. Tape it inside the box. Wrap the other end of the string with tape to make a nozzle. Tuck it into the other hole when it's not in use.

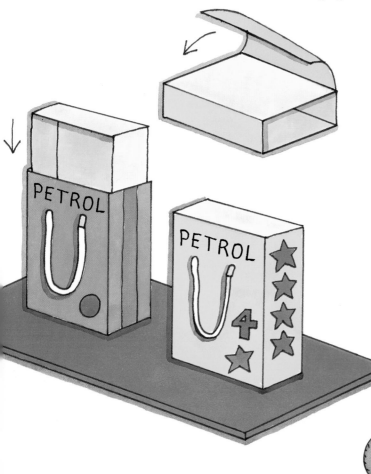

Decorate the pump, then push the drawer back in and glue your pump on to a piece of card. Make several, and stand them in front of your garage.

Car wash

This would look really fun next to your garage!

Cut three lengths of cardboard tube, about 10 cm long. Cover them with brightly coloured fun fur fabric.

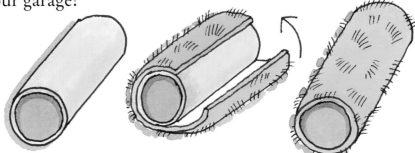

Make a simple frame with a strip of cardboard. Make sure your strip is narrow enough to fit through the tubes.

Thread the tubes on to your frame. Glue the frame to a cardboard stand.

Other buildings

Use different-sized boxes to make shops, a school, restaurants, and houses.
  Decorate them with pictures and write the names. Place them along the sides of the road.

Traffic jam frieze

Make a wall frieze to decorate your bedroom.

Cut a strip of paper or thin card about 15 cm high and as long as you like. (You could stick several pieces together to make a REALLY long one!)

Paint a black line along the bottom, for the road. Make it wavy if you like.

Follow the instructions on page 3 to make lots of car and truck shapes from the stencil sheet.

You can trace shapes directly on to your frieze, or make cut-out shapes first. Stick them in position after you have coloured them.

Paint the shapes, or colour them with crayons or felt-tips.

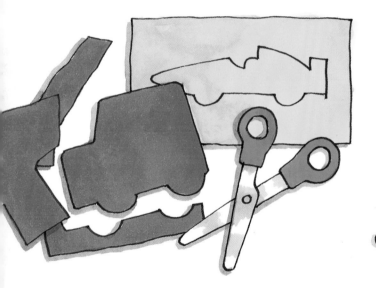

Turn the stencil over to get the vehicles going the other way.